PIANO ZEN

BY MARK HARRISON

PLAYBACK+
Speed • Pitch • Balance • Loop

To access audio visit:
www.halleonard.com/mylibrary

Enter Code
7520-6156-3828-3878

ISBN 978-1-70510-428-6

Visit Hal Leonard Online at
www.halleonard.com

Contact us:
Hal Leonard
7777 West Bluemound Road
Milwaukee, WI 53213
Email: info@halleonard.com

In Europe, contact:
Hal Leonard Europe Limited
42 Wigmore Street
Marylebone, London, W1U 2RN
Email: info@halleonardeurope.com

In Australia, contact:
Hal Leonard Australia Pty. Ltd.
4 Lentara Court
Cheltenham, Victoria, 3192 Australia
Email: info@halleonard.com.au

INTRODUCTION

Welcome to *Piano Zen*, the art of playing peaceful, relaxing music. Here, the term "Piano Zen" refers to a genre of piano music described as "Calm Piano," a meditative piano style that has its origins in the New Age genre, first popularized by George Winston in the 1980s. Fast forward to the 2020s, and we see this resurging in popularity, with artists such as Yiruma, Ludovic Einaudi, and Paul Cardall leading the way. We'll look at the styles of these artists and others, as we develop the approach in this book.

In here, we'll help you improvise your own calm piano pieces, starting with the basics and then adding more techniques as you progress. Along the way, you're always encouraged to experiment when composing and improvising.

At the end of the book, we have five complete pieces in the calm piano styles of various noted artists, which I hope will inspire your creativity in this genre. Good luck with *Piano Zen*!

– Mark Harrison

ABOUT THE AUDIO

On the accompanying audio tracks, you'll find recordings of all the music examples in the book. All the piano tracks feature the left-hand part on the left channel, and the right-hand part on the right channel, for easy hands-separate practice. The Piano Pieces in Chapter 7 have two audio tracks each: one solo piano as above, and the other with a light backing track on the left channel, and the piano part on the right channel. (This allows you to mute the right channel and play along with the backing track as desired.) All this is designed to give you maximum flexibility when practicing!

ABOUT THE AUTHOR

Mark Harrison is a professional keyboardist, composer/arranger, and music educator/author based in Los Angeles. He has recorded three albums as a contemporary jazz bandleader (with the Mark Harrison Quintet) and performs regularly throughout Southern California with the Steely Dan tribute band Doctor Wu. Mark's TV music credits include *Saturday Night Live*, *American Justice*, *Celebrity Profiles*, *America's Most Wanted*, *True Hollywood Stories*, and many others. Mark is an endorsed artist/educator for Dexibell keyboards, performing at the world-renowned NAMM music industry trade show in Los Angeles.

Mark has held faculty positions at the Grove School of Music and at the University of Southern California (Thornton School of Music). He runs a busy online teaching studio, catering to the needs of professional and aspiring musicians worldwide. Mark's students include Grammy winners, hit-song writers, members of the Boston Pops and L.A. Philharmonic orchestras, and first-call touring musicians with major acts. He has written over 30 music instruction books, as well as various Master Class articles for *Keyboard Magazine* and other publications.

For further information on Mark's educational products and on-line lessons, please visit www.harrisonmusic.com.

Chapter 1
WHAT IS PIANO ZEN?

As mentioned in the Introduction, here we're using the term "Piano Zen" to reference the Calm Piano genre. This is most often performed as a solo piano style, although light ambient backing tracks can sometimes be added, as for our Piano Pieces in Chapter 7.

We'll start out by learning some simple chord progressions, and see how to use "arpeggios," playing the notes of a chord one-at-a-time in a broken-chord style. This is central to a lot of Calm Piano music, and will be a foundation for you to start improvising your own progressions, in major and minor keys.

Then we'll develop techniques for creating melodies in this style, to go with the chord progressions as above. Our harmonies will start out with simple triads (three-part chords), and then move on to four-part (or "seventh") chords afterward. Along the way, we'll work with the typical rhythms in this style, both in 4/4 (four beats per measure) and 3/4 (three beats per measure) time signatures.

Later in this book, we'll introduce more advanced Calm Piano techniques such as combined arpeggios between the hands, 16th -note melodies, multiple "parts" within each hand, and so on.

The emphasis here is for you to start playing and improvising as soon as possible, without a whole lot of theory getting in your way! However, you'll see some Theory Tips in various places in this book, which you can read and use as desired. Occasionally these Tips will refer you to some of our other books, if you would like more detailed information on particular topics.

Now it's time to get started with some triad patterns in the right hand. On with the show!

Chapter 2
TRIAD PATTERNS FOR THE RIGHT HAND

(All the audio tracks in this chapter have the left-hand piano part on the left channel, the right-hand part on the right channel, and the click track in the middle. For examples with only a right-hand or left-hand part, this part is on both channels.)

Let's start out by playing a simple C major triad (three-note chord) as follows:

AUDIO TRACK 1

This is a common chord in all contemporary styles, including Calm Piano.

THEORY TIP: This triad is created from the 1st, 3rd, and 5th degrees of a C major scale. The "C" above the staff is a **chord symbol**, which denotes a C major triad.

Next we'll develop one of the most important Calm Piano techniques, the arpeggio pattern. This occurs when we play the notes of a chord one-at-a-time in succession, rather than all together as in Track 1 above. Here's an arpeggio pattern applied to the previous C major triad:

AUDIO TRACK 2

On the audio track you'll hear a count-in of four beats, followed by the C major arpeggio pattern as above. Notice that the notes of the chord blend together due to the use of the **sustain pedal**, which is a critical tool in Calm Piano styles. In most Calm Piano situations, you'll need to **depress** the sustain pedal for the duration of each chord, in order for the notes of the chord to blend together – and then release the sustain pedal when the chord changes. More about this later.

THEORY TIP: The 4/4 time signature signifies "four beats per measure," which is the most common time signature in Calm Piano. The **quarter-notes** in the first two measures, last for one beat each.

Next we'll get the left hand involved. The bottom (lowest) note of the C major triad we played in Tracks 1 and 2, is called the root of the chord. This can be played in a lower octave in the left hand, to support our right-hand arpeggio pattern:

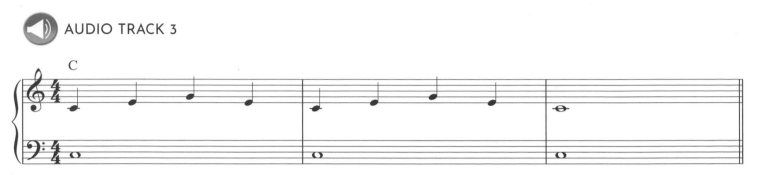

Again, the sustain pedal would normally be required, as you can hear on the audio track. (This is so typical of Calm Piano styles that pedal markings are not shown on the music.)

You can hear that this left-hand root note gives good fundamental support for the C major chord, below the right-hand part.

Our next step is to add eighth-note rhythms to our right-hand arpeggios. Eighth-note arpeggios are also common throughout Calm Piano styles:

THEORY TIP: The **eighth-notes** in the first two measures last for half a beat each.

Now it's time to develop some chord progressions, in the key of C major. If we're in the key of C major, this means that we hear the note C as the tonic or "home-base," and that we're staying within the restrictions of a C major scale. The C major triad we saw earlier is just one of the commonly used triads (three-part chords) available in the key of C:

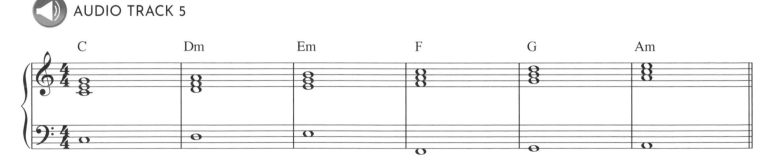

We can use any or all of these triads, when creating a progression in the key of C.

THEORY TIP: Musicians refer to these triads as being **diatonic** to the key; i.e., all the above triads are diatonic to (contained within) the key of C major. The chord symbols with the "m" suffix denote minor triads; i.e., **Dm** denotes a D minor triad.

Next we'll create a chord progression from these triad options, with eighth-note arpeggios in the right hand:

🔊 AUDIO TRACK 6

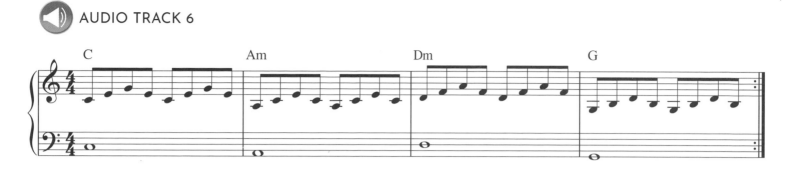

This progression started with the **C major triad** (the "home-base" chord) and then used other chords available in the key. When you play this example (or listen to the audio), you'll hear that as the progression is repeated, the tonic (home-base) of C is established. Many Calm Piano progressions will use the tonic chord of the key in this way.

Of course, this wasn't our only chord progression option from the choices in Track 5. Here's another example, again starting with the C major triad, using different chords:

🔊 AUDIO TRACK 7

Now it's your turn to improvise your own progression! For now, we'll keep the C major chord at the start of the four-measure phrase, to help establish the key. On the audio track, you'll hear the C major arpeggio pattern in the first measure (like the last two examples), but the piano will then drop out for the next three measures, leaving just the click track to play along with. As the track is repeated, you'll again hear the C major pattern at the start, and so on.

Go ahead and experiment with the different triad choices shown earlier. Here are some of the various possibilities you can try:

C–F–Am–G

C–Dm–Em–F

C–F–Dm–Am

and so on.

🔊 AUDIO TRACK 8

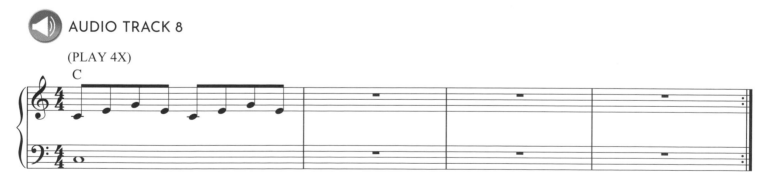

THEORY TIP: The Play 4X means that the four-measure progression plays four times in total on the audio track. You have four passes to insert your own chords in the empty measures shown above.

Of course, there's no rule saying that we have to play the C major chord at the start (or every four measures) of our progression: this was simply a training-wheels practice track to get us started. Now apply this arpeggio pattern to your own sequence of triads in the key of C major. (See Track 5 for your chord choices.) Experiment and enjoy!

While the previous chord patterns sound good, you may have noticed that (depending on the progression chosen) the right-hand range can jump around somewhat, resulting in transitions between chords that may not be as smooth as we would like. This is because all the right-hand triads so far have been in **root position**, meaning that the root of each triad has been the lowest note each time.

Next we'll see how to **invert** these triads to connect more smoothly between chords.

THEORY TIP: To **invert** a triad is to re-arrange the order of notes, from bottom-to-top. Using **inversions** to connect smoothly between chords, is known as **voice leading** in musician circles. Most popular piano styles (including Calm Piano) make use of voice leading between chords.

Here's how each of the commonly used triads in C major (from Track 5), can be inverted:

AUDIO TRACK 9

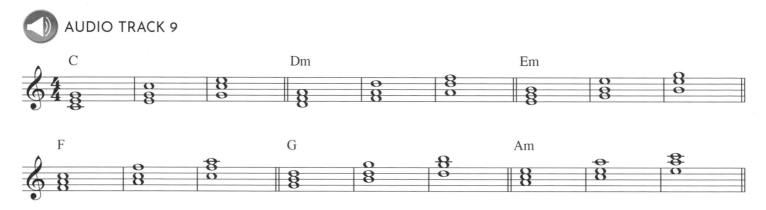

Now let's revisit the progressions we played earlier, this time using inversions to more closely connect between chords, keeping the eighth-note arpeggio pattern. First we'll apply inversions to the progression from Track 6:

AUDIO TRACK 10

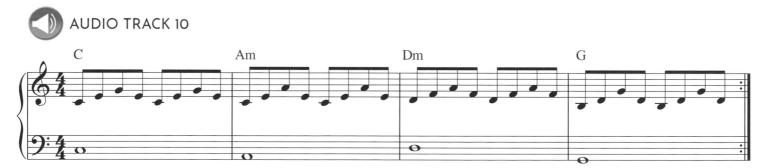

You can hear that the transitions between chords are more musical and connected by using inversions in this way. This is an important skill for you to learn! Next we'll apply inversions to the progression from Track 7:

AUDIO TRACK 11

When you're comfortable with these triad inversions, try using them when improvising your own progressions in the key of C; keep an eye on how closely the right hand is moving from one chord to the next. Again, you can use the earlier Track 8, starting with the C major chord for each four-measure phrase, to practice this if you like!

Next, we'll explore some right-hand patterns in the key of C minor, while also introducing 3/4 time, a staple of modern Calm Piano styles.

THEORY TIP: The 3/4 time signature signifies "three beats per measure." While not commonly used in mainstream pop styles, this time signature is often found in Calm Piano music.

We'll start out by building a simple C minor triad as follows:

AUDIO TRACK 12

This looks similar to the C major triad we saw earlier in Track 1, except the **third** of the chord (the middle note above) is now **flatted** to become E♭. You might hear the minor triad as having a darker or mellower quality compared to the major triad. Such impressions are subjective, of course!

Let's develop an arpeggio pattern for this C minor chord, in 3/4 time signature and with eighth-note rhythms, as follows:

AUDIO TRACK 13

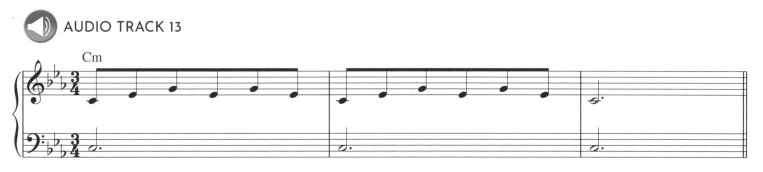

THEORY TIP: We now have a **key signature** (three flats) at the beginning of the music, indicating we are in the key of C minor.

It's time to develop a few chord progressions in the key of C minor. We'll still hear the note C as the tonic ("home-base"), but we'll be staying within the restrictions of a C natural minor scale overall.

The C minor triad above is just one of the commonly used triads (three-part chords) available in the key of C minor, as follows:

AUDIO TRACK 14

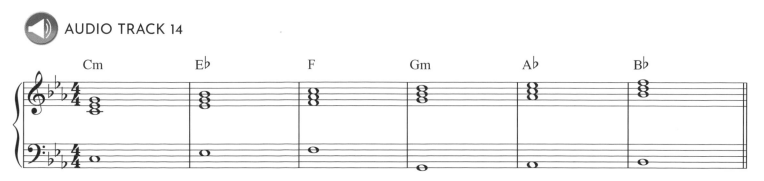

When creating a progression in the key of C minor, we can use any or all of these triads. Next, we'll create a chord progression from these options, with eighth-note arpeggios in 3/4 time, and with two measures for each chord:

AUDIO TRACK 15

Again, we've started with the "home-base" triad of C minor, then used other chords available in the key. When the progression is repeated, this helps to establish the overall key of C minor. As we have only three beats per measure, we're staying on each chord for two measures before moving to the next chord. This creates a more relaxed feeling typical of Calm Piano styles.

THEORY TIP: Musicians use the term **chord rhythm** to describe how often the chords change within a progression (i.e., once per measure, once every two measures, etc.).

Here's another progression example, again starting with the C minor triad, now using different chords from the available options in Track 14:

AUDIO TRACK 16

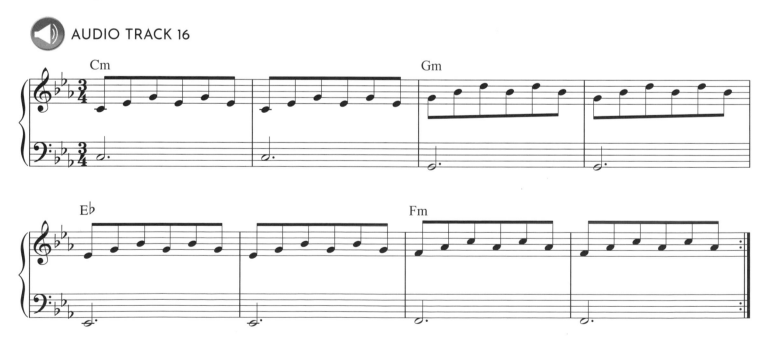

Next, you can improvise your own progression in this minor key. For now, we'll keep the C minor chord at the start; on the audio track, you'll hear the C minor arpeggio pattern in the first two measures (like the last two examples), but the piano will drop out for the next six measures, leaving just the click track to play along with. Then as the track is repeated, you'll hear the C minor pattern at the start, and so on.

Again, feel free to experiment with the different triad choices shown earlier, for the key of C minor. Here are some of the possibilities you can try:

Cm–A♭–E♭–Fm
Cm–B♭–Fm–E♭
Cm–Fm–Gm–E♭
and so on.

🔊 AUDIO TRACK 17

Again, there's no rule saying we have to play the tonic chord at the start of our minor key progression, so go ahead and apply this 3/4 arpeggio pattern to your own sequence of triads in the key of C minor. (See Track 14 for your chord choices.) Experiment and enjoy!

Similar to what we did earlier in the key of C major, we'll now see how to invert these triads in the key of C minor, to connect more smoothly between chords. The commonly used triads in C minor can be inverted as follows:

🔊 AUDIO TRACK 18

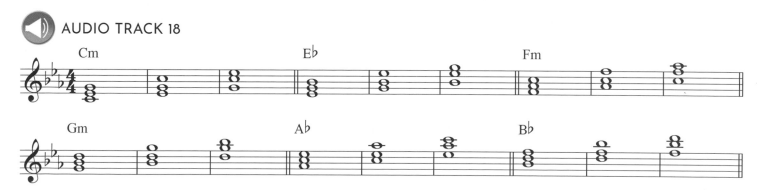

Now let's revisit the minor key progressions we developed earlier, this time using inversions to connect between chords more closely. First we'll apply inversions to the progression from Track 15:

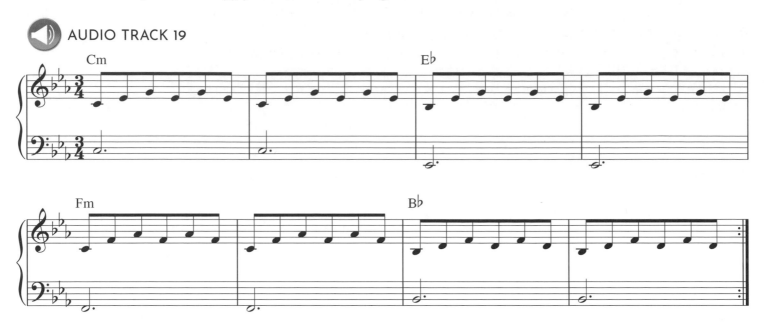

AUDIO TRACK 19

Again, the transitions between chords are more musical and connected when using inversions in this way. Next, we'll apply inversions to the progression from Track 16:

AUDIO TRACK 20

When you're comfortable with these triad inversions in the key of C minor, try using them when improvising your own. You can use Track 17, starting with the C minor chord for each eight-measure phrase, to get started with this as desired. Have fun!

THEORY TIP: for more information on triads and inversions, chord symbols, major and minor keys and key signatures, diatonic chords, and other basic theory topics – please refer to our book **Contemporary Music Theory, Level 1** (HL00220014) published by Hal Leonard.

Chapter 3
TRIAD PATTERNS FOR THE LEFT HAND

(All the audio tracks in this chapter have the left-hand piano part on the left channel, the right-hand part on the right channel, and the click track in the middle. For examples with only a right-hand or left-hand part, this part is on both channels).

In this chapter, we'll start to build triad patterns and arpeggios in the left hand. This is a staple technique in today's Calm Piano styles.

First, let's form a simple F major triad in the bass clef:

🔊 AUDIO TRACK 21

THEORY TIP: This triad is created from the 1st, 3rd, and 5th degrees of an F major scale.

Next, we'll play this chord with an eighth-note arpeggio pattern:

🔊 AUDIO TRACK 22

As usual in Calm Piano styles, we'll need to depress the sustain pedal for the duration of each chord.

THEORY TIP: We refer to left-hand arpeggio patterns as **closed** if they are within a one-octave range (as above), and **open** if they extend beyond an octave (more about these later in this chapter). **Closed** left-hand arpeggios are normally played around the top of the bass clef range, for clarity and to avoid muddiness.

The F major triad in Tracks 21-22 is just one of the common triads available in the **key** of F major:

🔊 AUDIO TRACK 23

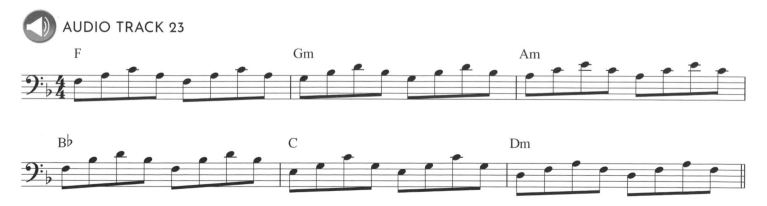

This example has a key signature (one flat) at the beginning of the music, indicating we are in the key of F major.

You'll see that we're using some triad inversions (re-ordering the sequence of notes, from bottom-to-top) for these arpeggios in the left-hand, to stay near the same register, just below the middle C area.

*Review the last chapter to see how to **invert** triads, as needed.*

Next, we'll develop some chord progressions in the key of F major, and create corresponding left-hand arpeggio patterns. For these progressions, we'll hear F as the tonic (home-base), and we'll be staying within the restrictions of an F major scale overall. Here's the first progression, with eighth-note arpeggios in the left hand:

AUDIO TRACK 24

This progression started with the F major triad (the "home-base" chord) and then used other chords available in the key. Again you'll hear that as the progression is repeated, the tonic ("home-base") is established – F, in this case.

Here's another example, again starting with the F major triad arpeggio in the left hand, now using different chords from the available options in Track 23:

AUDIO TRACK 25

Now let's see if you can create your own progression from these chords. Again, to help establish the key, we'll begin with the F major chord. On Track 26, you'll hear the F major arpeggio pattern in the first measure, but then the piano will drop out for the next three measures, leaving just the click track to play along with. As the track is repeated, you'll hear the F major pattern at the start, and so on.

Feel free to experiment with the different triad choices shown earlier, and to use different inversions of these triads to move more closely between chords. Some of the possibilities you can try are:

F–Dm–Gm–C
F–B♭–Am–Gm
F–Am–Dm–B♭
and so on.

AUDIO TRACK 26
(PLAY 4X)

As we saw in the Chapter 2 examples, we don't have to start a progression with the tonic chord (e.g., F major in the key of F), though this often occurs in Calm Piano and other styles. Go ahead and apply this type of arpeggio pattern to your own sequence of triads in the key of F major. (See Track 23 for the most common chord choices.) Feel free to experiment!

So far in this chapter, all the left-hand triad arpeggio patterns can be referred to as closed, meaning they are within a one-octave range. Now it's time to introduce some open triad arpeggios, which extend beyond a one-octave range. This is a vital left-hand technique in Calm Piano styles and contemporary ballad styles in general. Let's first look at a left-hand open-triad arpeggio pattern for an F major chord:

AUDIO TRACK 27

You can hear the broad, rich sound created with this left-hand pattern, which starts with the root and 5th of the chord (F and C), followed by the 3rd (A) up in the next octave. As usual, you'll need to depress the sustain pedal for the duration of the chord.

Don't try to stretch the overall span of this pattern in your left hand, which is not practical for many players. The sustain pedal is already holding the sound for you, so just play the notes individually while moving the hand up the keyboard. I recommend 5-2-1 fingering for the left hand (i.e., pinkie, index, thumb) for each ascending arpeggio in the preceding example.

Let's apply this new left-hand pattern to another four-measure progression in the key of F major:

AUDIO TRACK 28

Next, we'll add some right-hand triads to this left-hand pattern. Here's a reminder of the commonly used triads in the key of F, this time shown in the treble clef:

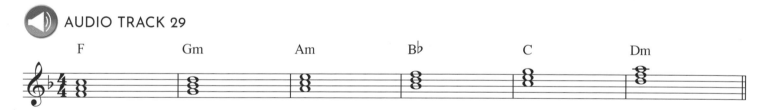

AUDIO TRACK 29

Now let's add the corresponding whole-note triads in the right hand, to the left hand open-triad arpeggios from Track 28:

AUDIO TRACK 30

Our next step is to use triad inversions, so we can move more closely between chords in the right hand. You can experiment with the order of notes within each triad (from bottom-to-top) to see what you like best. Here's one option, using inversions of the A minor and B♭ major triads in the right hand, for a smoother connection as we repeat the progression:

AUDIO TRACK 31

For this last variation on this progression, we'll split the right-hand triads in the second half of each measure. This involves playing the outer notes of each triad first, followed by the inner (middle) note. This works great with triads in all inversions. Just don't forget the sustain pedal.

AUDIO TRACK 32

Experiment with your own triad progressions using this technique!

Next, we'll look at some other left-hand patterns, and combinations with right-hand techniques, in the styles of iconic Calm Piano artists.

First, let's check out a left-hand pattern in the key of D major, in the style of Ludovico Einaudi and others. This pattern uses **syncopation**, where some of the left-hand notes land ahead of the beat. Played gently and with sustain pedal, this creates an interesting effect:

AUDIO TRACK 33

THEORY TIP: This example has multiple parts on the same staff – the half notes with downward stems, and the syncopated rhythms with the upward stems.

This progression also uses **bass inversions**, where chords are inverted over their 3rds or 5ths in the bass. For example, the chord symbol **A/C♯** denotes an A major triad placed over its 3rd (C♯) in the bass. Bass inversions are often used to create a smooth, melodic motion in the bass line.

Add some whole-note triads in the right hand to the above left-hand pattern:

AUDIO TRACK 34

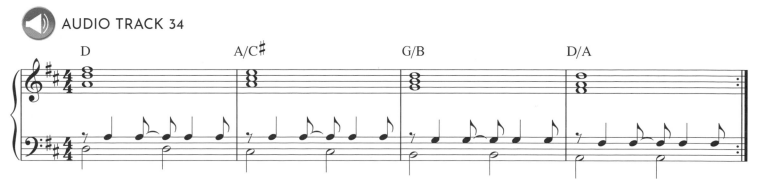

Here's one more variation of this example, with an eighth-note right-hand triad arpeggio at the end of each measure:

AUDIO TRACK 35

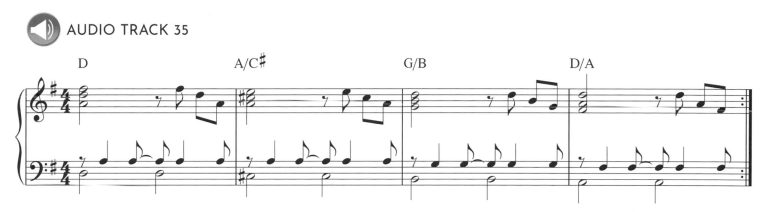

Next, we'll look at combining left-hand and-right hand arpeggios together, in the style of Paul Cardall and others. The following arpeggio pattern starts in the left hand, then continues in the right hand, before returning to the left hand. This enables the combined arpeggio pattern to have a larger continuous range. It is a useful textural effect, as shown in this eight-measure example in the key of B♭:

AUDIO TRACK 36

Remember to depress the sustain pedal during each chord, releasing exactly at the point of chord change, then depressing promptly during the next chord, and so on. All the triads in Track 36 are diatonic to (in the key of) B♭ major.

Next up is a useful variation of this two-handed pattern, using a different progression in the key of B♭, and *adding 9ths* to each of the chords:

THEORY TIP: We can often add a **9th** (equivalent to a whole-step above the root) to a major or minor chord in Calm Piano styles (and pop styles in general). This works best when the 9th of the chord is **diatonic** to the key, as in the example above.

To conclude this chapter, we'll look at a left-hand pattern in the key of D minor, in the style of Yiruma and others. This pattern uses only roots and 5ths of various chords, which results in a transparent, hollow effect. As always, play it gently and use the sustain pedal.

In Chapter 4, we'll work on adding right-hand melodic ideas over various left-hand progressions. For now, we'll preview a simple right-hand part added to the left-hand pattern above, playing the tonic of the key (D, in this instance) in octaves. This will add subtle coloring to the various chords available within the key.

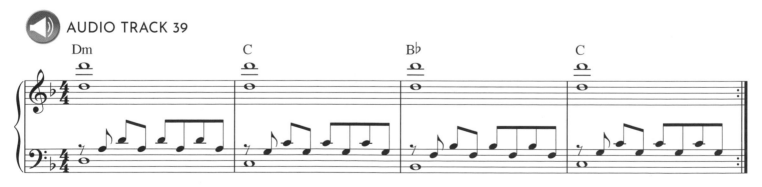

This is a good start to improvising some right-hand ideas over minor-key progressions. On to the next chapter, where we'll explore right-hand melody parts in more detail!

Chapter 4

CREATING MELODIES IN THE RIGHT HAND

(All the audio tracks in this chapter have the left-hand piano part on the left channel, the right-hand part on the right channel, and the click track in the middle. For examples with only a right-hand or left-hand part, this part is on both channels.)

In this chapter, we'll see how to create melodies in the right hand and combine them with various chordal patterns in the left hand. As a foundation for the first few melody examples, let's create left-hand **open-triad** arpeggio patterns based on the common chords in the key of G major:

🔊 AUDIO TRACK 40

THEORY TIP: All of these triad arpeggios are created from the root, 3rd, and 5th of their respective chords, **opened up** to create a range greater than an octave. See Tracks 27-32 in Chapter 3.

Next, we fashion a four-measure progression from these triads in the key of G, using this left-hand arpeggio pattern. Here is one of many chord progression options:

🔊 AUDIO TRACK 41

We'll now use this sequence as a structure over which we can begin improvising some melodic ideas. Using the 5th degree of a major key (D is the 5th degree of G major) in the melody is a great starting point, as this note will sound good over all the common triads shown above. Let's try it, using simple whole-note rhythms in the right hand, over the previous left-hand pattern:

🔊 AUDIO TRACK 42

You'll hear this has a tranquil and static effect, with the melody note D creating interesting vertical intervals against the root of each chord in the left hand.

Staying with whole-note rhythms in the right hand, let's use the tonic of the key (G in this case) as a melody note. This works over most of the chords available in the key. The next melody example alternates between the tonic (G) and 5th (D) of the key, using the same progression:

AUDIO TRACK 43

Our next step is to add the second degree of the major key (A is the 2nd degree of G major) to our melody note options. This is another note that fits over all the common triads in the key.

Now we'll add more rhythmic activity in the melody, with dotted-half notes and quarter notes:

AUDIO TRACK 44

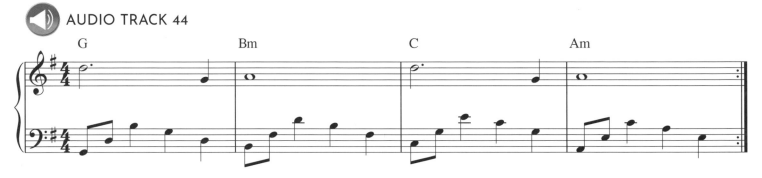

There are a lot of melodic possibilities using only these three notes. Feel free to experiment!

Take a look at the pentatonic scale, which is quite useful for creating Calm Piano melodies:

AUDIO TRACK 45

G pentatonic scale

THEORY TIP: The G pentatonic scale is created from the 1st (tonic), 2nd, 3rd, 5th, and 6th degrees of a G major scale; i.e., G, A, B, D, and E.

You can see that the previous melody notes G, A, and D are present in this scale, and that the notes B and E are now added.

Our next melody example includes all five notes in this G pentatonic scale, and adds more half-note and quarter-note rhythms:

Now it's time to experiment with your own right-hand melodies over this progression! You can play along with the left-hand pattern in Track 41, while going through the following steps:

- start with the 5th degree of the key (D) as in Track 42, varying the rhythms by ear as desired

- then expand to include the tonic (G) as well as the 5th (D) as in Track 43, again varying the rhythms as desired

- then you can add the second degree (A) as in Track 44, and then the other scale degrees in G pentatonic as in Track 46

Now you're ready to create your own progression from the diatonic triad left-hand patterns in G (from Track 40), and to begin creating your own right-hand melody over this, using the steps and techniques above. Use your ears to decide what works and what doesn't. Above all, have fun!

Next, we'll look at melody development in the key of G minor, while also exploring 6/8 time, which is another commonly used time signature in Calm Piano styles.

As a foundation for the following examples, let's create left-hand arpeggio patterns in 6/8 time, using the common chords in the key of G minor:

AUDIO TRACK 47

THEORY TIP: These triad arpeggios make use of **inversions**, to stay in the same range and to facilitate **voice leading** (close connection between chords).

THEORY TIP: Most 6/8 styles have two main pulses (or "big beats") per measure, falling on the **first** and **fourth** eighth notes. For that reason, on the click and count-off for this audio track, you'll hear an extra emphasis on these beats.

Let's devise an eight-measure progression from these triads in the key of G minor, with this left-hand arpeggio pattern. In 6/8 time, we'll often stay on the same chord for two or more measures, before moving to the next chord, for a more relaxed harmonic impression. Here's one of many progression possibilities we have from the above options:

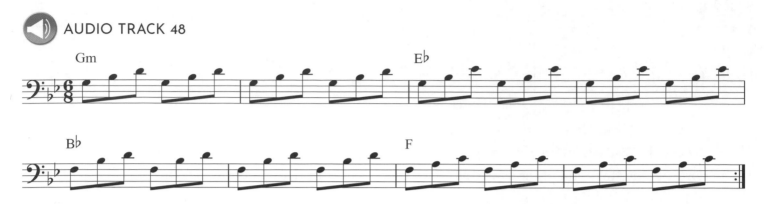

AUDIO TRACK 48

Again, we can begin improvising a few melodic ideas over this sequence, in the key of G minor, by using the 5th degree of the key (D). In the right hand, we'll use octave intervals that, with the sustain pedal, will project a pleasant "bell-like" quality:

AUDIO TRACK 49

As with the earlier major-key example, listen to the impression the repeated melody note D creates, against the changing harmonies in the left hand.

Now let's use the tonic (G) as a melody option in this minor key. Like the 5th degree (D), this note also works over the different chords available:

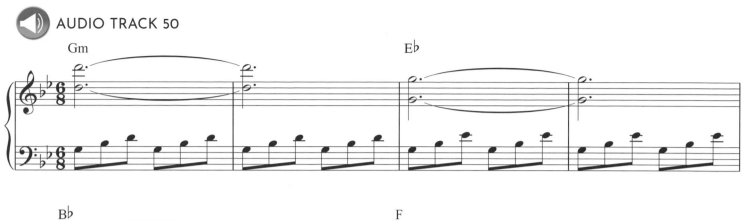

Our next step will be to add the 4th degree of the minor key (C is the 4th degree of G minor). This is another note that fits over the common triads in the key. We can also create more rhythmic activity in the melody by using dotted-quarter notes:

As before, the continuous octaves in the right-hand melody imparts a bell-like quality that is useful in Calm Piano styles.

Next, we'll introduce the **minor pentatonic scale**, which is commonly used in Calm Piano and other styles:

AUDIO TRACK 52

G minor pentatonic scale

THEORY TIP: The G minor pentatonic scale is created by taking a Bb pentatonic scale and re-positioning it to start on G, the 6th degree of a Bb major scale.

You can see that the previous melody notes G, C, and D are present in this scale, and that the notes Bb and F have been added.

The following melody example includes all five notes in this G minor pentatonic scale, and adds more melodic rhythms:

AUDIO TRACK 53

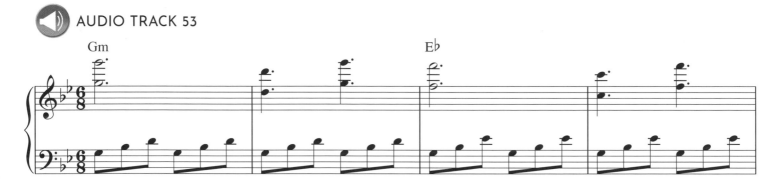

As before, you're encouraged to experiment with your own right-hand melodies over this minor-key progression. You can play along with the left-hand pattern in Track 48, while going through the following steps:

- start with the 5th degree of the key (D) as in Track 49, varying the rhythms by ear as desired

- then expand to include the tonic (G) as well as the 5th (D) as in Track 50, again varying the rhythms as desired

- then you can add the 4th degree (C) as in Track 51, and then the other scale degrees in G minor pentatonic as in Track 53

Create your own progression from the left-hand patterns in G minor (in Track 47), and begin creating your own right-hand melody over this, using the steps and techniques above. As always, trust you ears and enjoy!

Next, we'll look at some other right-hand melody techniques, combined with various left-hand patterns, in the styles of noted Calm Piano artists.

First, let's check out a busier melodic motif using an A pentatonic scale, in the style of Ludovico Einaudi and others. This melody displays consecutive eighth-notes and gentle syncopation:

AUDIO TRACK 54

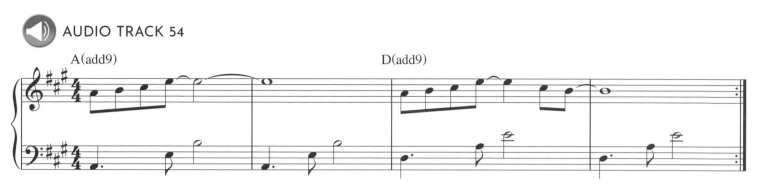

THEORY TIP: The left-hand arpeggio uses the root, 5th and 9th of each chord. This creates a modern, transparent sound well-suited to Calm Piano styles. The chord symbol suffix "add9" indicates that the 9th has been added to each chord.

As always in this style, depress the sustain pedal for the duration of each chord!

Take pentatonic melody ideas such as these and harmonize them with other chords available within the key (A major in this case). For example, here's the same pentatonic melody, now harmonized with B minor and F# minor chords, employing a similar left-hand pattern:

AUDIO TRACK 55

Next up is a melodic motif using a B natural minor scale, in the style of Yiruma and others. This melodic pattern starts on the 5th degree of the key (F#), then ascends one scale degree and down two scale degrees, in a repeated rhythmic pattern. This type of motif has various chord harmonization options within the minor key, as shown here:

AUDIO TRACK 56

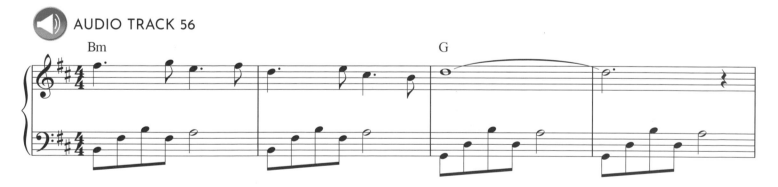

Note the interval movement in the left-hand pattern on beats 2 and 3 of each measure, which creates a simple counterpoint to the right-hand melody.

Have fun starting this type of right-hand melody idea at different points within the minor scale, harmonizing it with different chords available in this key. As always, use your ears!

On to another melodic idea in the style of Calm Piano artist Dustin O'Halloran and others. Here, the harmony is moving between minor triads in different keys, subjectively creating an unsettled feeling. The melody begins in A minor, but its notes are then altered to accommodate the following F minor chord:

AUDIO TRACK 57

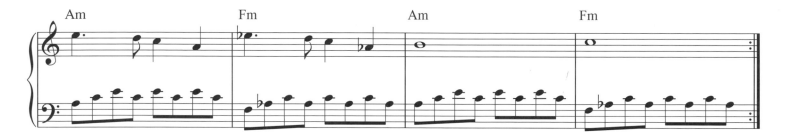

When you're ready, try out your own melodic ideas over this "A minor to F minor" progression. Ensure that the melody notes conform (i.e., are not dissonant) with the harmony.

Lastly in this chapter, we'll look at a rhythmic melody in the key of G, in the style of Paul Cardall and others. This melodic pattern uses notes within the G pentatonic scale (from Track 45), this time with eighth-note anticipations (landing ahead of the beat) for more rhythmic interest. By contrast, the left-hand accompaniment uses whole-note voicings, so as not to intrude on the right-hand rhythms:

AUDIO TRACK 58

THEORY TIP: In measure 5, we have a **Cmaj7** chord, with the left hand playing the root, 3rd and 7th. More about these four-part chords in Chapter 5.

THEORY TIP: In measure 6, we have a **Dsus** (suspended) chord. This is a D major triad in which the 3rd (F♯) has been **replaced** with the 4th (G).

After you've played through Track 58, experiment with your own right-hand melody ideas using the G pentatonic scale, over these chord changes (which are ubiquitous in Calm Piano styles). Have fun!

THEORY TIP: For more information on minor scales and keys, relative major and minor, suspensions, pentatonic scales, and other theory points mentioned in this chapter, please refer to **Contemporary Music Theory Level One** (HL00220014) and **Level Two** (HL00220015), published by Hal Leonard.

Chapter 5
USING FOUR-PART (OR "SEVENTH") CHORDS

(All the audio tracks in this chapter have the left-hand piano part on the left channel, the right-hand part on the right channel, and the click track in the middle. For examples with only a right-hand or left-hand part, this part is on both channels).

All the music examples so far in this book, except for Track 58, have used triad harmony; in other words, the progressions have consisted of three-part chords. This is the simplest and most common foundation for Calm Piano and other contemporary styles.

However, some Calm Piano pieces make use of four-part chords, which create a denser and more sophisticated effect.

THEORY TIP: Four-part chords are sometimes referred to as "seventh chords," as most (but not all) of them contain a 7th – in addition to a root, 3rd, and 5th.

We'll start out with a couple of four-part chord examples in the left hand:

AUDIO TRACK 59

Note that each of these chords has a root, 3rd, 5th, and 7th. Playing these four-part chords in the left hand will sound muddy if played too low. The C major 7th chord in this example is near the bottom of the useful range.

Let's combine these two chords into a progression, in the key of E minor. First, create a simple eighth-note arpeggio pattern in the left hand:

AUDIO TRACK 60

As usual in this style, remember to depress the sustain pedal for the duration of each chord, releasing the pedal at the point of chord change.

Next, we'll work on some right-hand melody ideas over this left-hand pattern, using the **E minor pentatonic** scale (shown here):

 AUDIO TRACK 61

As we saw in the last chapter, the minor pentatonic scale is a staple melodic technique in Calm Piano styles.

THEORY TIP: The E minor pentatonic scale is created by taking a G pentatonic scale and re-positioning it to start on E, the 6th degree of a G major scale.

For the next example, pick out some whole notes from this scale in the right hand, and use them over the left-hand arpeggio pattern from Track 60, like this:

AUDIO TRACK 62

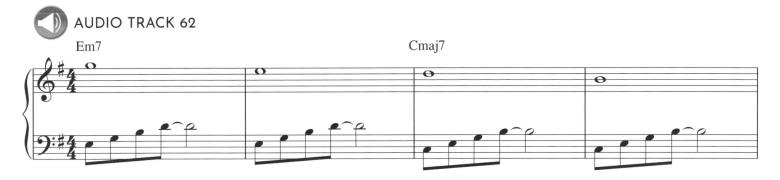

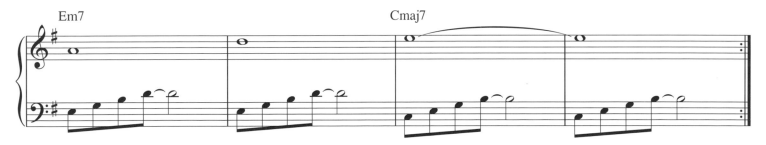

On to our next left-hand pattern over these changes. We can create a more "open" harmonic sound by using only the root, 5th, and 7th of each chord, in the style of Yiruma and others:

AUDIO TRACK 63

Add a right-hand melody line over this left-hand pattern, still within the E minor pentatonic scale, but now with octaves and more rhythms:

AUDIO TRACK 64

On to our next technique: mixing these left-hand, four-part chords with the triads and inversions seen in earlier chapters. Here's a simple left-hand sequence in the key of A, combining four-part Dmaj7 and F#m7 chords with an Esus (E suspended triad) and A major triads, in the style of Paul Cardall:

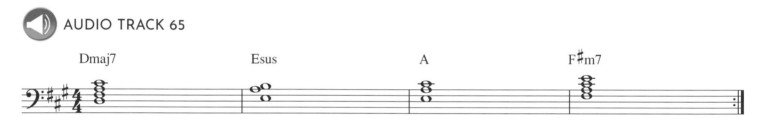

AUDIO TRACK 65

THEORY TIP: The Esus (E suspended triad) is created by taking an E major triad and replacing the 3rd (G#) with the 4th (A). This is a common sound in Calm Piano styles.

This type of static left-hand part (just whole notes) can work well with a right-hand melody that has more subdivisions and/or anticipations (notes landing ahead of the beat).

Now use this left-hand part with a right-hand melody created from an A pentatonic scale:

AUDIO TRACK 66

The A pentatonic scale is created from the 1st (tonic), 2nd, 3rd, 5th, and 6th degrees of an A major scale: A-B-C#-E-F#.

We've already seen that the pentatonic scale is a frequent melodic source in Calm Piano styles, as it can often "float over" the different harmonies available.

Next, try a different melodic motif over these same chords, again within an A pentatonic scale restriction, and using the same rhythm:

🔊 AUDIO TRACK 67

Now it's your turn to experiment with a few melodies over this progression, using the notes within the A pentatonic scale, as above. You can start out by play along with the left-hand pattern in Track 65, while trying out your right-hand melodic ideas. Then when you're ready, take over the left-hand part and make the progression your own!

Our next example using four-part chords is in 3/4 time, reminiscent of film composer Joe Hisaishi's more tranquil and relaxing side. First, let's create a simple eight-measure chord progression in the left hand, back in the key of C:

🔊 AUDIO TRACK 68

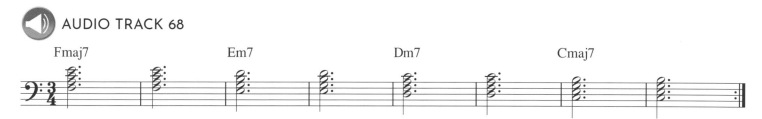

Do you hear the fuller, denser sound created by these four-part chords, as opposed to the triads we've used in earlier examples?

Next we'll add a simple melody on top of these chords, in the right hand. This melody is derived from the C pentatonic scale, as follows:

🔊 AUDIO TRACK 69

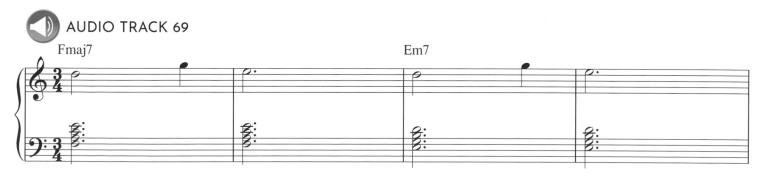

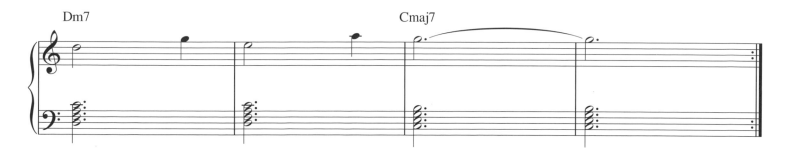

Now it's time to embellish and develop this melody idea as follows:

- In the left hand, split up the dotted-half-note voicings, with the root of the chord on beat 1, and the rest of the chord (3rd-5th-7th) on beat 2 of each measure
- In the right hand, add eighth-note fills at the end of each two-measure phrase for a busier effect:

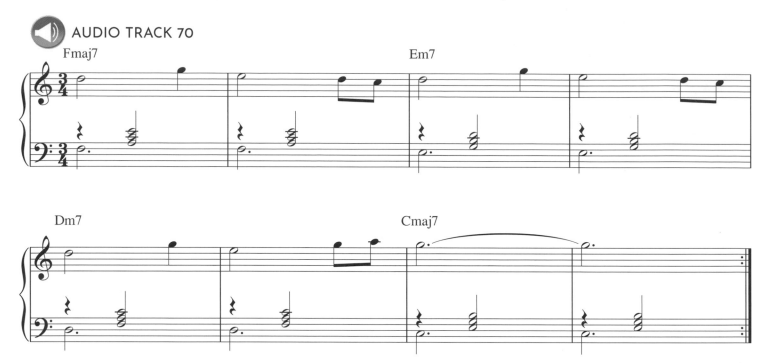

We can develop this melody arrangement even further, as follows:

- In the left hand, play on all three beats in each measure (root on beat 1 and the other chord tones, 3rd-5th-7th, on beats 2 and 3), creating a gentle waltz effect
- In the right hand, add more eighth-notes from the C major scale, rather than be restricted to C pentatonic:

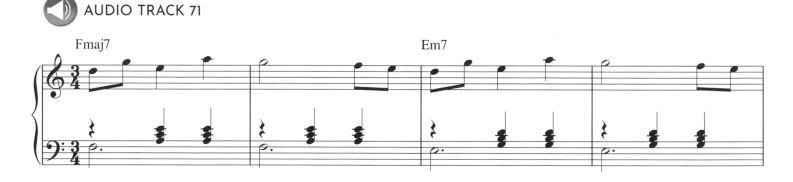

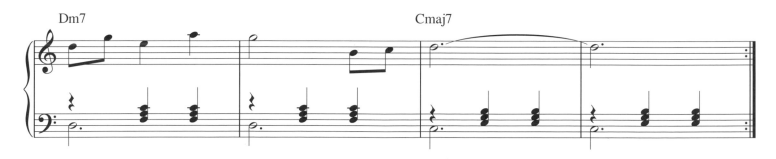

THEORY TIP: The C pentatonic scale consists of the notes C, D, E, G, and A. The above example adds the remaining notes within the C major scale (F and B) back into the mix.

Some caution may be needed when using all the melody notes within a major scale in this way, as tensions can occur between the melody and the chord being used – which may be undesirable in Calm Piano styles. As always, use your ears, and have fun experimenting!

Our final example with four-part chords in this chapter uses more sophisticated harmony in the style of Yiruma and others. We'll start out with a four-measure chord progression in G minor, and the following left-hand arpeggio pattern:

🔊 AUDIO TRACK 72

THEORY TIP: The Am7(♭5) and D7 form a "two-five" progression; these chords are built from the 2nd and 5th degrees in the key of G minor. This is a cornerstone of jazz harmony and is sometimes heard in more advanced Calm Piano styles.

Now we'll try some melodic ideas over this progression, using the **G natural minor** scale, the most commonly used minor scale in contemporary styles. In case you're unsure about the notes in this scale, here's a quick review:

🔊 AUDIO TRACK 73

Next, we add a simple melody on top of the chord pattern in Track 72, in the right hand. This melody is derived from the G natural minor scale:

🔊 AUDIO TRACK 74

There are many right-hand melody options (within the G natural minor scale) over this progression! The following example adds more melodic movement and rhythmic subdivision to the right-hand melody:

🔊 AUDIO TRACK 75

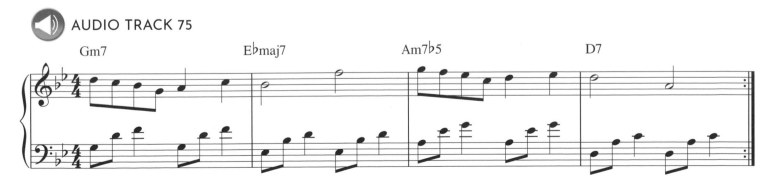

Go ahead and experiment with your own melodies over this progression, in G minor. You should strive to create melodies that are memorable and stand up on their own, yet sound harmonious (i.e., not dissonant) with the chord progression. Have fun!

THEORY TIP: For more information on four-part chords, progressions in minor keys, "two-five" progressions, and other theory points mentioned in this chapter, please refer to **Contemporary Music Theory Level One** (HL00220014) and **Level Two** (HL00220015), published by Hal Leonard.

Chapter 6
MORE ADVANCED TECHNIQUES

(All the audio tracks in this chapter have the left-hand piano part on the left channel, the right-hand part on the right channel, and the click track in the middle. For examples with only a right-hand or left-hand part, this part is on both channels).

This chapter explores some of the more evolved melody and harmonization techniques used by noted Calm Piano artists.

First we'll see a left hand device that splits a left hand-triad arpeggio, in the style of Phillip Glass and others. The lowest note in the left hand is held (sustained), while the upper notes alternate in an eighth-note rhythm, as in the following example:

AUDIO TRACK 76

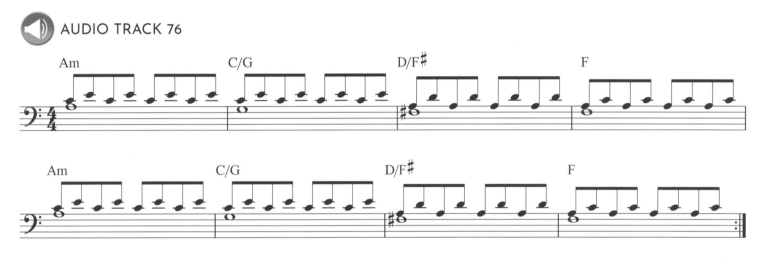

Using high-register octaves with a sparse rhythm is an effective right-hand melody technique. Take a look at the following example:

AUDIO TRACK 77

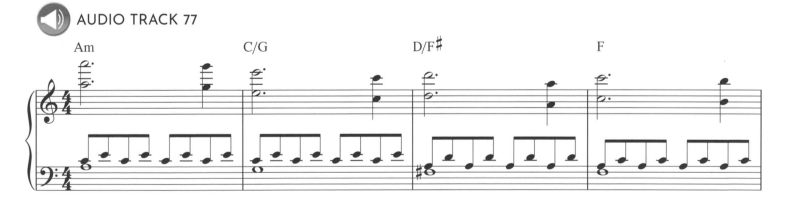

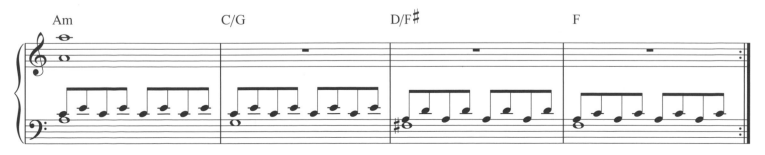

THEORY TIP: This progression is in the key of A minor, with melody notes derived from the A natural minor scale.

For another more textural option, create an arpeggio pattern in the right hand, using just the tonic (A) and 5th (E) of the minor key. These notes will float over all the chords used in this progression:

AUDIO TRACK 78

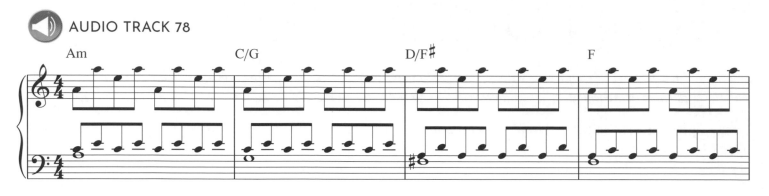

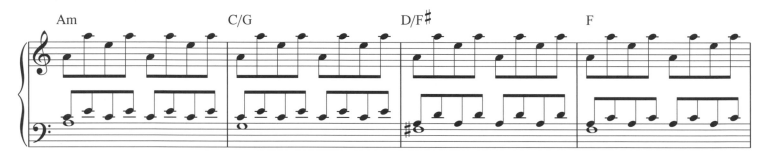

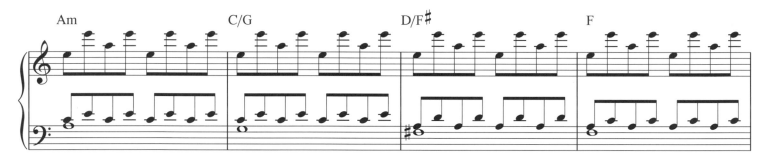

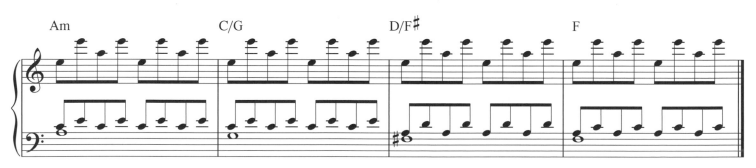

We've used a contrasting right-hand arpeggio approach for each half of this example, as follows:

- In the first half (measures 1-8), the tonic of the key (A) is played in octaves throughout, except for the 5th of the key (E) on beats 2 and 4 of each measure.

- In the second half (measures 9-16), the 5th of the key (E) is played in octaves throughout, except for the tonic of the key (A) on beats 2 and 4 of each measure.

This is a fun progression to create a right-hand part over. Play along to the left-hand pattern in Track 76, improvising your own melody or pattern ideas!

Now let's add some intervals below a melody in the right hand. This is a staple piano ballad technique across the range of contemporary styles. The 6th is the most common interval to add below melody in Calm Piano styles, due to its broad and consonant quality.

First, we'll develop a left-hand arpeggio pattern with added 9ths, in the style of Yiruma and others:

AUDIO TRACK 79

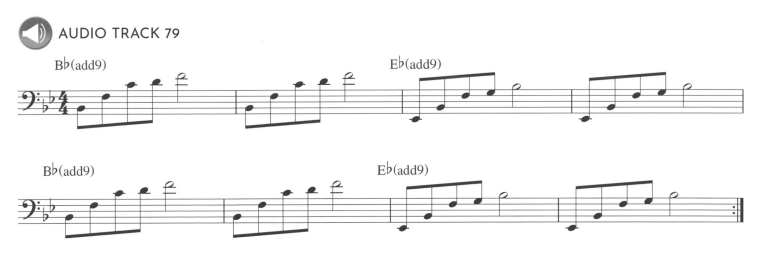

Next, we'll develop a melody in the key of B♭, to go over this left-hand pattern, with 6th intervals added below the melody in the right hand.

For example:

- the first melody note is D, so we add F below (6th interval below D)

- the next melody note is C, so we add E♭ below (6th interval below C)

- and so on.

All the added notes below the melody will also belong to the B♭ major scale, shown here:

AUDIO TRACK 80

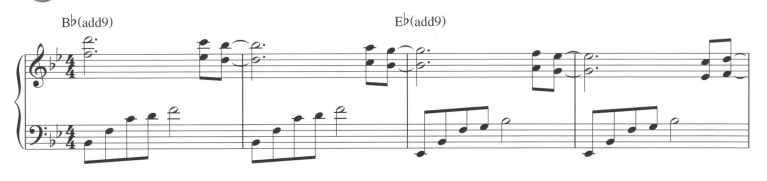

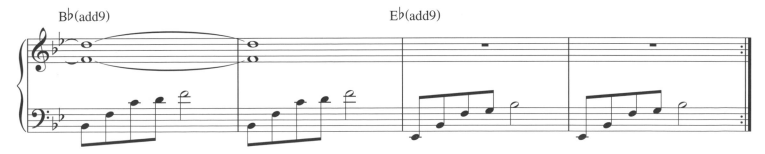

This is fun! Let's create another melody over these changes. As before, start on D and add 6th intervals below, this time using a repeated dotted-quarter-note rhythm in the melody:

AUDIO TRACK 81

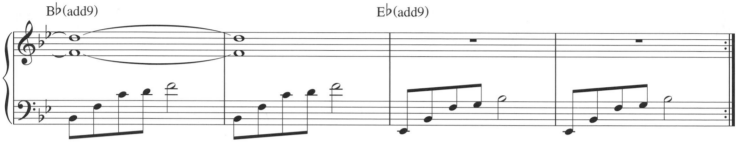

THEORY TIP: This type of repeated rhythm figure (i.e., consecutive melody notes lasting for one-and-a-half beats each, across multiple measures) is sometimes referred to as **rhythmic displacement**. This is a common technique in various contemporary styles.

Now let's learn how to fashion a left-hand melody line within a 16th-note arpeggio pattern, in the style of Einaudi and others. This requires good dynamic control between the hands: the right-hand part needs to be played more quietly, to allow the moving line in the left hand to take center stage:

AUDIO TRACK 82

THEORY TIP: This example is in the key of A minor, and the tonic of the key (A) is used as a repeated note on all the chord changes, a common Calm Piano technique.

Let's devise a variation for this left-hand melody. Try this one:

AUDIO TRACK 83

Okay! Now it's your turn to experiment with various left-hand melody notes, within this pattern!

Earlier, we saw how to create combined arpeggio patterns between the left hand and right hand. Next, in this more advanced setting, we'll see how to add a right-hand melody part on top of this two-handed arpeggio approach, in the style of Paul Cardall and others.

This technique requires the right hand to play two parts at the same time: the main melody on top (at a higher dynamic level) and the arpeggio tones below (at a lower dynamic level). Apply this to a simple melody in the key of D minor:

Lasty in this chapter, we'll explore the use of repeated eighth-note triads and suspensions below the melody in the right hand, in the style of Einaudi and others. Together with the sustain pedal, this device can create an insistent and hypnotic effect that is useful in Calm Piano styles.

In the following example, a melody moving by 2nds is harmonized by repeated eighth-note chords in the right hand:

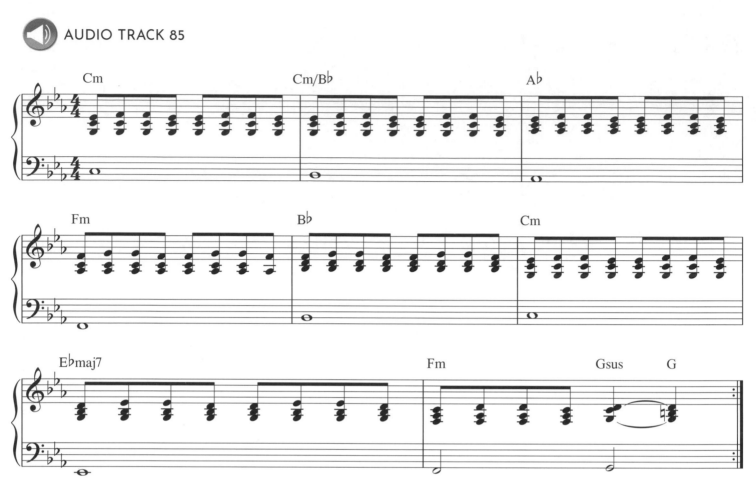

AUDIO TRACK 85

This is just a sampling of the many possibilities available within Calm Piano styles. These are great ways to dress up your own melodies and improvisation ideas. Good luck – and have fun!

Chapter 7
PIANO PIECES

(All the examples in this chapter have two audio tracks. One has the left-hand piano part on the left channel, the right-hand part on the right channel, and the click track in the middle. The other has a backing track on the left channel, and the piano part on the right channel, so you can mute the right channel to play along with the backing track).

This chapter features five complete pieces in the style of noted Calm Piano artists.

The first is cast in the style of "Fly" by Ludovic Einaudi, in 4/4 time.

Piece #1

AUDIO TRACKS 86 / 87

Moderately slow (♩ = 75)

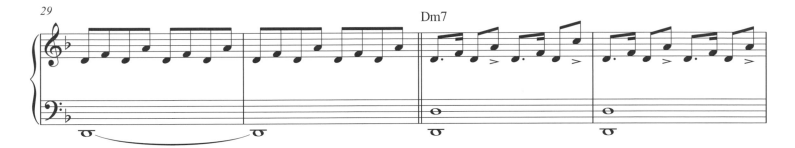

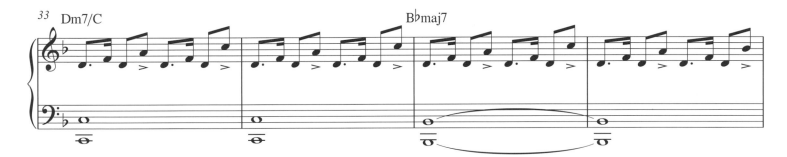

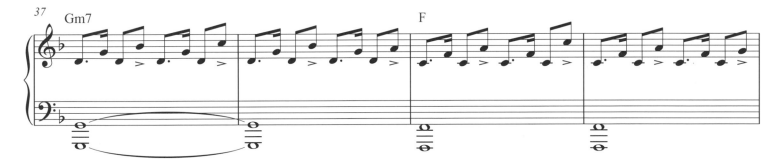

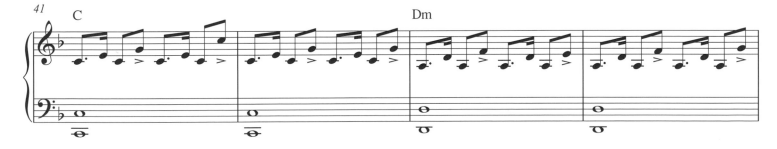

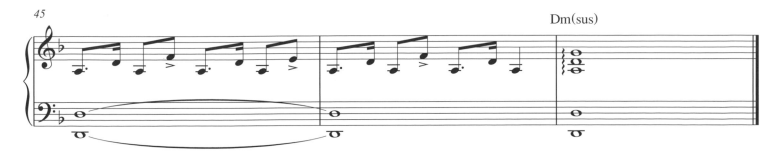

Next, we have a piece that evokes the style of "Kiss the Rain" by Yiruma, also in 4/4 time.

Piece #2

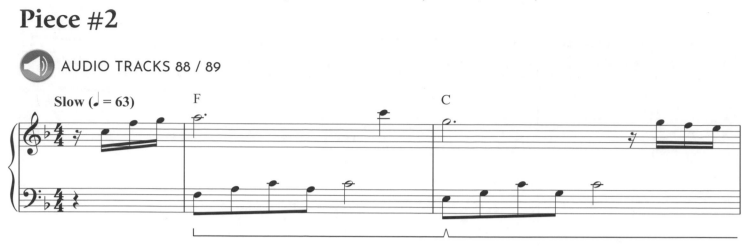

AUDIO TRACKS 88 / 89

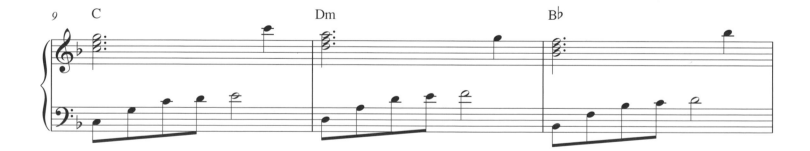

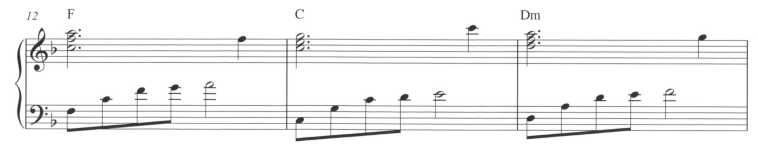

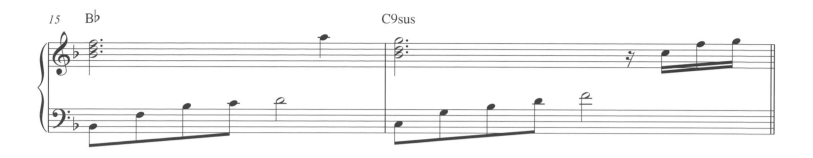

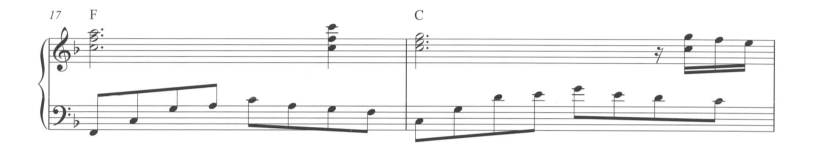

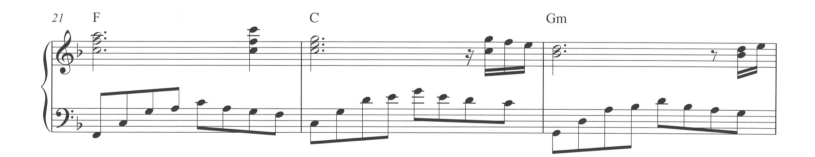

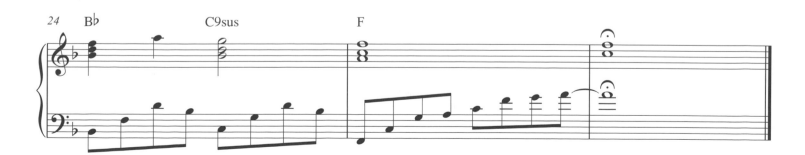

The following piece is in the style of "Prelude No. 2" by Dustin O'Halloran, also in 4/4 time.

Piece #3

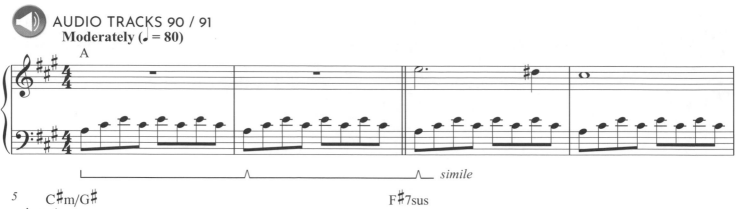

AUDIO TRACKS 90 / 91
Moderately (♩ = 80)

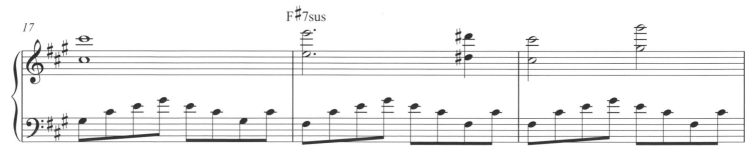

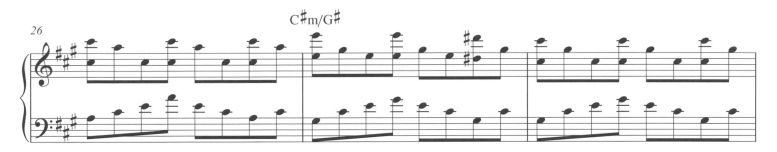

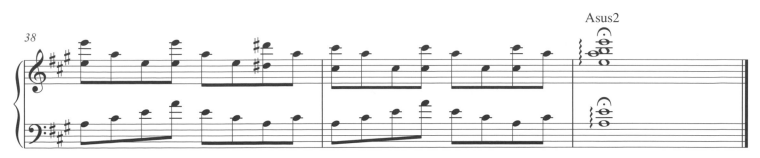

The next piece is set in the style of "Indaco" by Ludovic Einaudi, in 3/4 time.

Piece #4

🔊 AUDIO TRACKS 92 / 93

Moderately (♩ = 85)

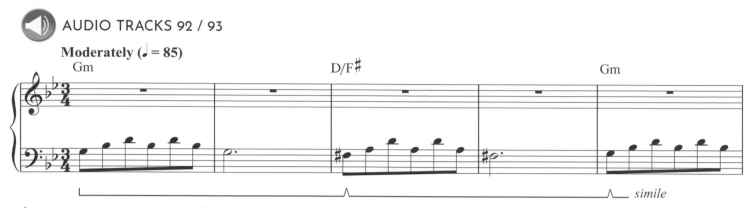

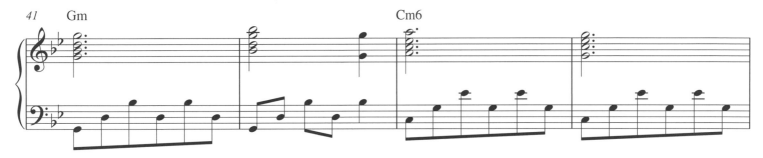

Finally, we have a piece in the style of "Dance of the Forgotten" by Paul Cardall, in 6/8 time:

Piece #5

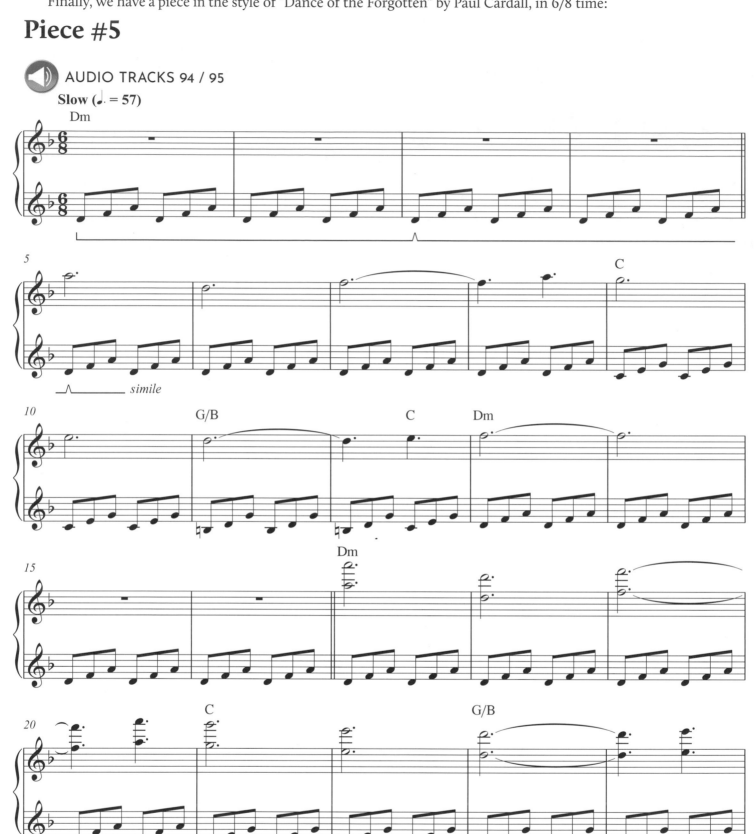

AUDIO TRACKS 94 / 95

Slow (♩. = 57)

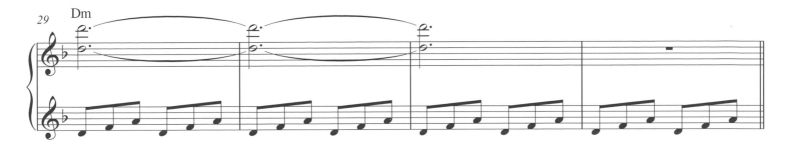

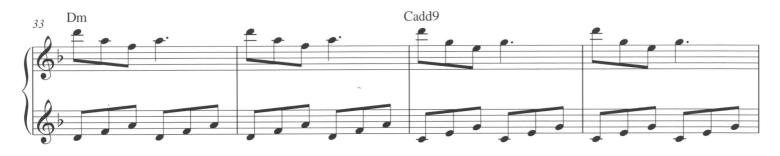

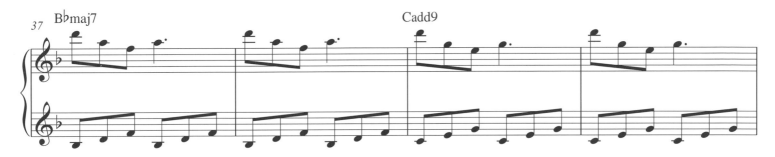

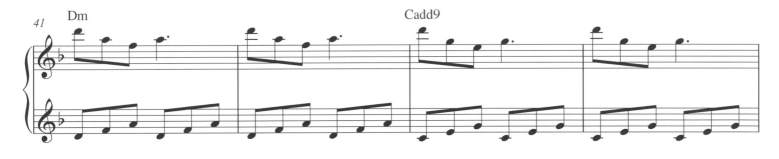

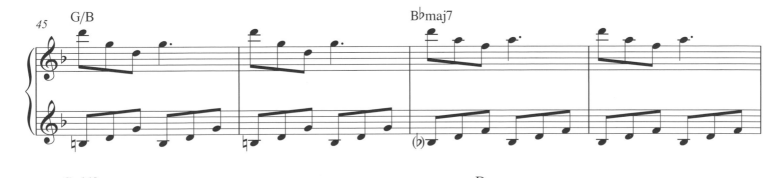

KEYBOARD STYLE SERIES

THE COMPLETE GUIDE!

These book/audio packs provide focused lessons that contain valuable how-to insight, essential playing tips, and beneficial information for all players. From comping to soloing, comprehensive treatment is given to each subject. The companion audio features many of the examples in the book performed either solo or with a full band.

BEBOP JAZZ PIANO

by John Valerio

This book provides detailed information for bebop and jazz keyboardists on: chords and voicings, harmony and chord progressions, scales and tonality, common melodic figures and patterns, comping, characteristic tunes, the styles of Bud Powell and Thelonious Monk, and more.
00290535 Book/Online Audio $18.99

BEGINNING ROCK KEYBOARD

by Mark Harrison

This comprehensive book/audio package will teach you the basic skills needed to play beginning rock keyboard. From comping to soloing, you'll learn the theory, the tools, and the techniques used by the pros. The accompanying audio demonstrates most of the music examples in the book.
00311922 Book/Online Audio $14.99

BLUES PIANO

by Mark Harrison

With this book/audio pack, you'll learn the theory, the tools, and even the tricks that the pros use to play the blues. Covers: scales and chords; left-hand patterns; walking bass; endings and turnarounds; right-hand techniques; how to solo with blues scales; crossover licks; and more.
00311007 Book/Online Audio $19.99

BOOGIE-WOOGIE PIANO

by Todd Lowry

From learning the basic chord progressions to inventing your own melodic riffs, you'll learn the theory, tools and techniques used by the genre's best practicioners.
00117067 Book/Online Audio $17.99

BRAZILIAN PIANO

by Robert Willey and Alfredo Cardim

Brazilian Piano teaches elements of some of the most appealing Brazilian musical styles: choro, samba, and bossa nova. It starts with rhythmic training to develop the fundamental groove of Brazilian music.
00311469 Book/Online Audio $19.99

CONTEMPORARY JAZZ PIANO

by Mark Harrison

From comping to soloing, you'll learn the theory, the tools, and the techniques used by the pros. The full band tracks on the audio feature the rhythm section on the left channel and the piano on the right channel, so that you can play along with the band.
00311848 Book/Online Audio $18.99

COUNTRY PIANO

by Mark Harrison

Learn the theory, the tools, and the tricks used by the pros to get that authentic country sound. This book/audio pack covers: scales and chords, walkup and walkdown patterns, comping in traditional and modern country, Nashville "fretted piano" techniques and more.
00311052 Book/Online Audio $19.99

GOSPEL PIANO

by Kurt Cowling

Discover the tools you need to play in a variety of authentic gospel styles, through a study of rhythmic devices, grooves, melodic and harmonic techniques, and formal design. The accompanying audio features over 90 tracks, including piano examples as well as the full gospel band.
00311327 Book/Online Adio $17.99

INTRO TO JAZZ PIANO

by Mark Harrison

From comping to soloing, you'll learn the theory, the tools, and the techniques used by the pros. The accompanying audio demonstrates most of the music examples in the book. The full band tracks feature the rhythm section on the left channel and the piano on the right channel, so that you can play along with the band.
00312088 Book/Online Audio $17.99

JAZZ-BLUES PIANO

by Mark Harrison

This comprehensive book will teach you the basic skills needed to play jazz-blues piano. Topics covered include: scales and chords • harmony and voicings • progressions and comping • melodies and soloing • characteristic stylings.
00311243 Book/Online Audio $17.99

JAZZ-ROCK KEYBOARD

by T. Lavitz

Learn what goes into mixing the power and drive of rock music with the artistic elements of jazz improvisation in this comprehensive book and CD package. This instructional tool delves into scales and modes, and how they can be used with various chord progressions to develop the best in soloing chops.
00290536 Book/CD Pack..........................$17.95

LATIN JAZZ PIANO

by John Valerio

This book is divided into three sections. The first covers Afro-Cuban (Afro-Caribbean) jazz, the second section deals with Brazilian influenced jazz – Bossa Nova and Samba, and the third contains lead sheets of the tunes and instructions for the play-along audio.
00311345 Book/Online Audio $17.99

MODERN POP KEYBOARD

by Mark Harrison

From chordal comping to arpeggios and ostinatos, from grand piano to synth pads, you'll learn the theory, the tools, and the techniques used by the pros. The online audio demonstrates most of the music examples in the book.
00146596 Book/Online Audio $17.99

NEW AGE PIANO

by Todd Lowry

From melodic development to chord progressions to left-hand accompaniment patterns, you'll learn the theory, the tools and the techniques used by the pros. The accompanying 96-track CD demonstrates most of the music examples in the book.
00117322 Book/CD Pack..........................$16.99

HAL•LEONARD®

Prices, contents, and availability subject to change without notice.

www.halleonard.com

POST-BOP JAZZ PIANO

by John Valerio

This book/audio pack will teach you the basic skills needed to play post-bop jazz piano. Learn the theory, the tools, and the tricks used by the pros to play in the style of Bill Evans, Thelonious Monk, Herbie Hancock, McCoy Tyner, Chick Corea and others. Topics covered include: chord voicings, scales and tonality, modality, and more.
00311005 Book/Online Audio $17.99

PROGRESSIVE ROCK KEYBOARD

by Dan Maske

You'll learn how soloing techniques, form, rhythmic and metrical devices, harmony, and counterpoint all come together to make this style of rock the unique and exciting genre it is.
00311307 Book/Online Audio $19.99

R&B KEYBOARD

by Mark Harrison

From soul to funk to disco to pop, you'll learn the theory, the tools, and the tricks used by the pros with this book/audio pack. Topics covered include: scales and chords, harmony and voicings, progressions and comping, rhythmic concepts, characteristic stylings, the development of R&B, and more! Includes seven songs.
00310881 Book/Online Audio $19.99

ROCK KEYBOARD

by Scott Miller

Learn to comp or solo in any of your favorite rock styles. Listen to the audio to hear your parts fit in with the total groove of the band. Includes 99 tracks! Covers: classic rock, pop/rock, blues rock, Southern rock, hard rock, progressive rock, alternative rock and heavy metal.
00310823 Book/Online Audio $17.99

ROCK 'N' ROLL PIANO

by Andy Vinter

Take your place alongside Fats Domino, Jerry Lee Lewis, Little Richard, and other legendary players of the '50s and '60s! This book/audio pack covers: left-hand patterns; basic rock 'n' roll progressions; right-hand techniques; straight eighths vs. swing eighths; glisses, crushed notes, rolls, note clusters and more. Includes six complete tunes.
00310912 Book/Online Audio $18.99

SALSA PIANO

by Hector Martignon

From traditional Cuban music to the more modern Puerto Rican and New York styles, you'll learn the all-important rhythmic patterns of salsa and how to apply them to the piano. The book provides historical, geographical and cultural background info, and the 50+-tracks includes piano examples and a full salsa band percussion section.
00311049 Book/Online Audio $19.99

SMOOTH JAZZ PIANO

by Mark Harrison

Learn the skills you need to play smooth jazz piano – the theory, the tools, and the tricks used by the pros. Topics covered include: scales and chords; harmony and voicings; progressions and comping; rhythmic concepts; melodies and soloing; characteristic stylings; discussions on jazz evolution.
00311095 Book/Online Audio $19.99

STRIDE & SWING PIANO

by John Valerio

Learn the styles of the stride and swing piano masters, such as Scott Joplin, Jimmy Yancey, Pete Johnson, Jelly Roll Morton, James P. Johnson, Fats Waller, Teddy Wilson, and Art Tatum. This book/audio pack covers classic ragtime, early blues and boogie woogie, New Orleans jazz and more. Includes 14 songs.
00310882 Book/Online Audio $19.99

WORSHIP PIANO

by Bob Kauflin

From chord inversions to color tones, from rhythmic patterns to the Nashville Numbering System, you'll learn the tools and techniques needed to play piano or keyboard in a modern worship setting.
00311425 Book/Online Audio $17.99